2017

Blessings!

[signature]

"BE GOOD!"

Raising Kids That You And Others Will Actually Want To Be Around

Tara R. Wells

WESTBOW
PRESS®
A DIVISION OF THOMAS NELSON
& ZONDERVAN

WestBow Press books may be ordered through booksellers or by contacting:

WestBow Press
A Division of Thomas Nelson & Zondervan
1663 Liberty Drive
Bloomington, IN 47403
www.westbowpress.com
1 (866) 928-1240

Because of the dynamic nature of the Internet, any web addresses or
links contained in this book may have changed since publication and may
no longer be valid. The views expressed in this work are solely those
of the author and do not necessarily reflect the views of the publisher,
and the publisher hereby disclaims any responsibility for them.

Any people depicted in stock imagery provided by Thinkstock are models,
and such images are being used for illustrative purposes only.
Certain stock imagery © Thinkstock.

ISBN: 978-1-5127-6062-0 (sc)
ISBN: 978-1-5127-6063-7 (hc)
ISBN: 978-1-5127-6061-3 (e)

Library of Congress Control Number: 2016917236

Print information available on the last page.

WestBow Press rev. date: 11/18/2016

FOREWORD

PRAISE FOR "BE GOOD!"

–A teacher's first-hand perspective–

As an educator for over 20 years, I have been blessed to have worked with so many wonderful children and their families. In my experience, a confident, persevering, empathetic, well-rounded student usually has a family that loves and guides their children with clear rules, rewards and consequences. What does this look like? Look no further! Take a peek into a household that is indeed filled with children you *want* to be around.

Tara Wells' book, "Be Good!" is a no-nonsense must-read for any parent with young ones. It contains a wealth of practical knowledge to get you through the younger years of your children. (I'm already looking forward to the sequel, "The Teenage Years"!)

—*Helen Villongco, Elementary School Teacher for 25 years, teacher to 3 Wells children, and mom to 2 amazing sons.*

Table of Contents

Dedicated to

Caden

Brady

Nathan

&

Ellie

The reasons

I want to be a

"good" mommy.

Fairy Tales Do Come True

Once upon a time, there was a little girl who loved all things tiny. Tiny animal and doll figurines (she collected 3 inch tall "Cabbage Patch Posable Figures" back when the craze started in the 80s), itty bitty critters like baby chicks and bunnies, teensy flowers (a.k.a. weeds) plucked out of the grass that could make bouquets for her Barbies and their tiny Barbie babies. All she wanted to do was take care of those teeny little tinies: Baby them, cradle them, feed them, nurture them, and love them.

The little girl dreamed of one day taking care of her own real, live, tiny babies. Once, she found a wounded baby bird in her back yard, and her mommy and daddy miraculously let her put it in a box, bring it into her room, and nurse it back to health with a medicine dropper and some seed meal. When the baby bird started growing into an ugly, gawky, freaky looking thing that pooped on her carpet and squawked all night long, she knew it was time to set it free. Did you know crows have the ugliest 2-week old babies on the planet?

As the girl grew, she continued wanting to baby all things tiny. When her sister called her soon after getting married (but before finishing college), hysterical because a little blue plus sign appeared on a stick, the little girl was ECSTATIC. A *real live baby* was coming soon for her to love! And when her niece was born and her sister came to visit at their parents' house where she still lived, she would sneak off into her room with that precious baby and pretend that gorgeous little girl was her own (you might think she was still a child herself, pretending to be a mommy, but no, she was now 22.)

Fast-forward a few years, and the girl found a husband who thought her obsessive, nurturing ways were somehow "cute", and they produced 4 little cooing babies to love in the span of 7 years: 3 little Blue Ones, and lastly a little Pink One too.

The girl was in sweet, maternal bliss. OK, bliss is an exaggeration. The girl was in a whirlwind of diapers, boo-boos, ba-bas, pacis, laundry, dishes, broken arms, black eyes (that year's Shutterfly album can confirm these details), poo-poos (the babies kept eating, and the overflow kept coming), more laundry (the babies are not known for their natural cleanliness, it turns out), and kisses and snuggles. Somehow, those last two made it all worthwhile.

You probably guessed it: That girl is me. Yes, 4 children later, my wish came true and it just kept a-comin'! My oldest is now 14, then 13, next 11, and the youngest is 7, and if I've done my math correctly, I have 45 years of parenting under my belt. As each child is entirely unique and requires at least a slightly different parenting approach, I'm counting all my years of parenting each of them separately. Bear with me on this one -- and if you have been blessed with more than one child, you will probably agree.

So what I want to share with you, and whatever parent decides to read this (probably on the pot with a kid banging on the door asking for a juice box), is that:

a.) it gets easier and more fun (*I promise*) and

b.) your kids can BE GOOD*.

Not all the time, of course (now what fun would that be? Then you'd never get to use your crazed, freaked-out mommy screech that made my oldest describe me as a "scary guy" once when he was 4). But they can *be good*, and the reward will be kids who you (and others!) will actually enjoy being around. With a Bachelor's degree in Psychology, a Master's in Time Out+, and Double-Doctorate in Laundry & Let The Punishment Fit The Crime+, I stand behind my methods. My hope is that you pick up a few nuggets for the parenting journey too!

---

* *I will define more in depth what "be good" means in the intro, but for now suffice it to say that I believe that all kids are good (amazing, in fact!). It's **behaviors** that need to be modified to help them to **behave appropriately**, or, for purposes of this book, to "be good".*
+ *You know I'm kidding, right? There's no such thing, but truly, most parents would agree there ought to be. I know I've earned mine multiple times over.*

INTRODUCTION

Why I Write

In the process of raising 4 kids, I've come across a lot of families: Families with both parents at home and families with just one. Families with healthy control over their brood and families who've lost or never had control (and who usually know it but don't know what to do about it). Parents who hover and parents who disengage. Parents who are mean and bossy, and parents who are pushovers. I've also spent my fair share of time fluctuating between the extremes of overly-controlling to far too lax, and I've watched my kids' behaviors follow suit.

I've spent countless hours observing other families, read thousands of words written by umpteen authors from all different parenting "camps", and sorted through what made sense, what seemed to work, and what had to be thrown out with the bath water (preserving the precious baby in the process!)

Ultimately, what I desired was to create a well-rounded environment for our kids to be brought up in: With an insane amount of love, affirmation, hugs, kisses, encouragement and praise, and with a fair measure of training, discipline, guidance, boundaries, and parameters too, giving them a clear path as to how to "be good".

I'm not an expert on parenting, any more than my dad, who doesn't have a degree in horticulture, is not an expert at gardening. But he grows the best tomatoes on the planet because:

1.) he's done his homework on what works, and

2.) he's grown tomatoes for a really long time, year after year, and has improved and modified his techniques over time to perfect his art.

Over the past 25-ish years of studying Psychology, teaching special needs and typical kids, observing (and living alongside) families with Little Ones, raising my own brood, and voraciously reading every book, magazine article, website, and proverb I could find on raising well-behaved kids who could "be good" (at least most of the time!), I realized that I was pulling what I call 'nuggets' from all of these resources, and tucking them away for use when needed.

I knew I wanted to raise kids who were kind, responsible, compassionate, respectful, and eventually independent. So early on (and with the help of older, wiser parents in my life), I identified 3 House Rules, defining for our family and setting the parameters for "being good" in our home:

1. **Be Kind (The Golden Rule)**
2. **Listen & Obey**
3. **No Grumbling & Complaining.**

Breach the rules, and you've strayed from the path of acceptable, or "good", behavior.

I knew training kids to live in these boundaries wasn't going to happen by accident. I believe all kids are amazing. *And all kids are also a work in progress.* They don't come automatically knowing how to "be good", and it was my job to ensure they knew what was expected of them. I learned that "good" parents set their children up for success by making expectations crystal clear, and using respectful tones and language to train their little moldable offspring. Lovingly guiding them into kind and respectful adulthood was (and continues to be) the ultimate goal.

Over the years I also began to see a common thread developing between my core belief system and my approach to child-rearing (and truly, all relationship-building). I believe there are **3 essential gifts** all humans are striving toward: **Love, Acceptance, and Belonging.** And the people (adults and children alike!) who were the healthiest, kindest, and most well-adjusted typically received all 3 of these in abundance along their journey. In turn, they were also freed to *give* these abundantly to those around them. These **3 gifts** are paramount in the methods and tactics I choose as I parent my brood. I'll expand on these in the final chapter.

Once my kids reached an age where we began circulating back into society after what felt like being home-bound for a lonnnnnng time due to years of pregnancy and morning sickness, nursing, sleep depravation, naps for babies, potty training, terrible-twos survival, etc., I started hearing compliments on our kids' behavior. Comments were coming from friends and strangers alike, questions from disheveled mommies on how I do it with 4 kids who seem to *listen*, and an uncanny amount of requests from friends and even acquaintances to "write a book" to share the nuggets I've learned (and kept tossing out there for these busy and often overwhelmed parents to catch).

Until now I didn't feel I had either the time or the qualifications to put anything truly helpful or useful on paper. But the nuggets are beginning to spill out of my brain and mouth (to many friend's and stranger's chagrin) at an uncanny rate these days, and it's time.

I received a bachelor's degree in psychology from UC Santa Barbara emphasizing child development. Although I came out of school a far cry from an "expert" in the field, it created in me a craving to know more, to read more, to study more, to learn more, and to be the best parent I could be when the time came for my husband and I to start our Baby Making factory, lovingly called the Wells Home. (Little did we know how productive our little factory was going to be!) And so, friends, here lies a compilation of the "nuggets of wisdom" I've gained, observed, and tried to apply - imperfectly, of course - as I parent my brood.

For what it's worth, I firmly believe that psychology

is just an observable and definable way to understand that the Greatest Psychologist, our Creator, installed in us the blueprints we need to learn and then teach our children healthy behaviors. And to modify our (and their) behaviors when boundaries are crossed and outcomes are less than optimal. Ultimately to be amazing parents, who train our precious Little Ones entrusted to our care, to *Be Good.*

CHAPTER 1

Who's The Boss?

Children come into this world with pretty reasonable expectations. When they cry, they are typically telling you one of four things: I'm hungry, I'm tired, something hurts, or I'd like a clean di-dee. Some experts in infant behavior have even learned to distinguish between the different cries of infants and can tell you from the tone and inflections of a particular cry which of these needs the child wants met! (Dunstan, Priscilla, 2012).

Ultimately, though, there is one expectation that the child has immediately upon arrival into the world: "Tell Me Who's Boss." This can also be translated as, "You know better than me, right? After all, I'm the

Newbie here!" Think of the way a baby looks up at Mommy's face with a look of complete and utter trust and expectation. Trust that she knows best. Expectation that she knows how to meet his needs. And she does!

We are all given instincts and wisdom that kicks into high gear when Baby arrives into our world, and we *do* know how to care for our precious Little Ones! We know with a certain degree of accuracy (and after just a little observation and practice) when he's hungry, tired, hurting, needs a paci, a diaper change, a snuggle or a nap. It's partly learned and partly instinctual. We know better than the little guy, because we've watched and learned from the wisdom of those who have parented before us, and we've also been wired by our Creator to take care of these precious Little Ones.

All aspects of child-rearing requires that the parents give their child the reassurance and comfort of knowing "I'm the boss." It's not out of the parent's desire or need to control, but rather out of an innate sense of knowing that "I have a lot of years on you, Little One, so trust me when I say that I know better than you!"

When mommy lays her Little One down for a nap and

he squirms, protests, and disagrees that it's actually time for rest, she can trust that she knows best. Infants need, on average, 15-16 hours of sleep a day! (Weissbluth, Marc, M.D., 1999). But some fiestier infants disagree, and when both the clock and the baby's signals tell mommy it's time for Little One to sleep, the infant fights it - especially if he's over-tired at this point. But, mommy knows best and she rocks, soothes (or attempts to soothe) and lays her baby down to sleep regardless of his disapproval of the plan. [For more specifics on helping your baby get on a routine, try reading my favorite book on establishing a predictable schedule: "Secrets of the Baby Whisperer" by Tracy Hogg, 2005.]

Thus, we as parents are given the profound authority and responsibility to take the reigns and teach our babies, with loving, gentle firmness, that we know how to take care of them. We've been given the high calling of doing that, regardless of what baby thinks should be going down. Some babies think nursing or sucking should happen 24/7. But speech therapists, orthodontists, and mommies who have been over-suckled will all agree that there is a limit to the amount of sucking that's healthy for a baby!

So step one to training our kids to be good is determining from the get-go that "I'm the boss". In our home, our kids know that:

1.) Mommy and daddy are in charge.
2.) God gave us that privilege and responsibility, and He expects us to follow through.

Have you ever spent time with a family where the kid was in charge? Although a tantrum may (or may not) have been temporarily avoided, there's a discomfort in just watching the scenario go down, recognizing that the parent is clearly not in charge:

Trying to make an exit from a playdate:

Mommy: "Pookie, it's time to go now...."

Pookie: "NO!!! I don't want to!"

Mommy: "Please don't say no to mommy, Pookie. We really have to leave now or we'll be late to pick up brother...."

Pookie: "NO! I don't want to go! It's not fair!!!"

Mommy: "But Pookie, we have to be on time to get brother from school, it wouldn't be fair to make him wait..."

Pookie: *"I DON'T WANT TO!"* (running away from Mommy).

Mommy: "OK, only a few more minutes though. I'll go find your shoes..."

Mommy is desperately trying to both please Pookie and avoid a conflict (i.e. a tantrum), but in doing so she is definitively telling her child that he is in control. *He* decides when the play date ends, *he* chooses when they leave and if it's a peaceful exit, and *he* dictates whether or not they are on time to pick up brother. That's a lot of control to give to a Little One! And he knows it. He doesn't want that control, in fact he fears that control because it means that the one who should know best is deferring to *him*!

So he begins to resent and defy his mommy even more, because he is looking for her to take charge, to be the boss, and to tell *him* the rules. She, however, is too concerned about his emotional outburst to meet his deeper need, which is to be taught boundaries, respect, self-discipline and obedience; Ultimately, to be taught that he is *not* the boss, and how to be good (and what that even means)!

How does he even know what "good" behavior is if it's not clearly laid out for him? Ironically, when Mommy approaches Pookie in 5 minutes to leave, it's almost certain that Pookie will tantrum at that point anyway. He already knows his emotional outbursts rock his Mommy, and he's going to use that to his advantage. So chances are she didn't actually avoid a conflict, she just postponed it.

There are many types of parenting styles, but according to Dr. James Dobson in *The New Dare to Discipline*, most fall into some sub-category of these three types: Authoritarian, Permissive and Authoritative.

Authoritarian parents, although intent on being the boss, take command of their Little Ones using whatever means necessary: anger, over-bearing power, and oftentimes unnecessary and harsh punishments. They believe that immediate obedience is the ultimate end-result, not guiding a child into respectful, responsible adulthood, and whatever method gets them there is a-okay. You've probably heard this type hollering at their child at the park for running away, or barking inappropriately at him in the grocery store when he grabs the cookies off the shelf. The child may (or may not) jump to respond and obey, but there's typically a lack of calm, peace, and respectfulness about the approach, along with fearfulness in the child of the parent. "Harsh", "controlling" and "critical" are descriptives commonly used for these parents.

Typically children raised in this environment are prone to either becoming extremely passive and fearful, or will learn to challenge, rebel against, and resent authority down the road.

Permissive parents are at the opposite end of the spectrum, who allow their children's wants and desires to dictate their own parenting decisions or lack of. They are often slow to respond to disrespectful or disobedient behaviors (they may claim "I don't want to damage his self-esteem!" or simply try to avoid conflicts or emotional outbursts), and who ultimately allow the child to be the boss. Permissive parents usually don't recognize or trust their own innate wisdom, may have lost it somewhere in their own upbringing from an overly harsh or permissive experience, or have such a mild temperament themselves that it feels "unnatural" for them to lead with confidence. They oftentimes claim that their child is the most strong-willed or defiant child you've ever met (and he's probably confirming that or *becoming* that because he's pushing at boundary lines that keep moving). Pookie's mommy is a good example of a permissive parent.

Children of permissive parents often believe they are - or should be - "the center of the universe", and become disdainful and resentful of authority. Eventually, they will begin acting out toward those closest to them.

Authoritative parents take a balanced approach to parenting where they believe that most often they know best, and have the confidence in themselves to follow through on the directives and instructions they give their child. They recognize that parenting carries with it a responsibility to raise respectful, compliant, thoughtful children, who are also kept safe by the boundaries they are setting. They typically use a loving but firm approach that tells the child in no uncertain terms that what they say will be obeyed, and if not, there will be a consequence. They use rewards (such as "Good job, Sweetie! I appreciate it when you listen the first time."), consistency, and both natural and disciplinary consequences to follow through when kids disobey.

Studies show that parents who take an authoritative approach typically raise children who are responsible, respectful, and trusting of authority (Dobson, 2012).

Here's an example of an authoritative parent:

> Mommy: "Sweetie, in 5 minutes we're going to leave."

> (5 minutes pass).

> Mommy: "Sweetie, it's time to go. We're leaving to pick up brother."

> Sweetie: "I don't want to go!!! I'm having fun with my BFF!"

> Mommy: "I know sweetheart, but we are picking up brother. Get your shoes on, they're by the door." (Taking child's hand and walking toward the door).

Sweetie: "I don't want to....."

Mommy: "I understand, but we're leaving." (Guides child to put shoes on.) "Good job getting your shoes on! Say good-bye and thank you to BFF and her mommy."

Child puts shoes on with mommy helping or guiding, says good-bye and mommy holds her hand as they walk to the car.

In this scenario, what works for this authoritative mommy is that she:

1. Gives the child a heads-up of what's to come.
2. Says what she means and both she and the child know it.
3. Follows through with action (taking her hand) when child doesn't listen to first request.
4. Gives positive reinforcement in complimenting the child's (guided) obedience in putting shoes on, and mild negative reinforcement by holding child's hand (she's lost a bit of freedom), assisting with shoes on, and holding her hand again to the car.

The mommy in the above scenario is implementing her authority without wielding it unnecessarily over her child. She is also resisting the temptation to be passive and avoid a potential argument by calmly and confidently taking charge, deciding what time is appropriate for them to leave. Both mommy and Sweetie know that mommy is in charge, and although Sweetie may want a different outcome, she probably also knows that fighting mommy isn't going to change anything, because she consistently follows through on what she says, and ensures her daughter is compliant.

If you have a defiant toddler, you may be thinking, "That would never work with my kid!" But if you begin the process of consistently being the boss early on (when the child is still an infant, with you determining naps, feeding times and schedules, and even giving short time-outs in the crib when tantrums or defiance begins around 9-12 months), the process is much smoother in the toddler years to getting them on board with recognizing boundaries and following directions.

If you're starting later, know that *it's never too late!* You can become the loving, respected leader of your home, starting now. It will take a little more time and diligence, but with consistently calm, loving, but firm control from you, it will happen. And your home will reap the rewards of being a more peaceful, compliant, and enjoyable place!

Follow Through To Show Who's Boss

Ensuring that your child follows through on your directives (and the instructions of the other adults in his life) is the simplest, most direct route to establishing yourself as your child's leader, or if you prefer, guide. If he doesn't respond to a request or command you've made the first time, it's time for you to *take action*.

When he's just an itty bitty guy (1 ½) and he's dumped all his blocks out, when it's time to put them away, you give him a cue (I like the "clean up" song our big purple dino friend taught us way back when), and then, hand-over-hand, guide the little guy to help put his blocks back in the bucket. It's a lot slower-going than just doing it yourself, but it also lays the ground work and establishes the expectation for him helping, learning responsibility, and following directions from you, down the road.

As he gets bigger, "time to get dressed!" doesn't always have to be a battle if you lead him into his room as you say it, and assist him in taking his jammies off and getting clothes on, even if he is resisting (hint: you're still a lot stronger and smarter than him at this point!). It's also a good idea to give him 2 choices of clothes to wear. This gives him the sense that he has some control, while avoiding him picking out the plaid shorts with the tye-died shirt, or battling you over what you've picked out.

The message here is simple: If he doesn't do it himself the first time (and rather quickly), the second request comes with you assisting him to do what he's been asked. It takes time from you (away from whatever else you were doing, of course), but sooner than later, the pay-off is your child responding to your requests right away. They don't particularly like being led and directed (we can relate, right?!), so he will learn that following orders beats mommy or daddy holding his hand or guiding him while he does it.

And you win, too! By around age 3, he's picking up his toys and getting dressed on his own. Of course, as he gets older he may refuse to obey, and a consequence is in order. We'll get to age-appropriate consequences in chapter 5.

A friend who also has 4 children just a bit ahead of mine gave me an invaluable nugget when my kids were tiny: At the onset of training Little Ones, *only give a command when your child is within arm's reach.* This allows you to immediately be hands-on if he doesn't comply, showing him hand-over-hand (your hands guiding his) how to follow through on the directive once its been given. This teaches them quick and "first time obedience", meaning when I say it, you do it (or I'll help you do it!).

This also means when they're a bit bigger and you have to begin giving commands from a distance, (like at the park when it's time to call them back to you), they will comply and come to you rather than run away. They've learned that following your requests is non-negotiable.

Recently, I told our (then) 6 year old daughter it was time for a bath. When I found her sitting on the couch with her brother a few minutes later watching a baseball game, I said, "Sweetheart, it's bath time *now.* If you're not in the tub in 2 minutes (the amount of time it takes her to run in there and dis-robe), you'll be in bed right after with no book." She was in tubby-time in 2 minutes flat.

Notice that follow-through does NOT come with nagging. Asking the child multiple times, or explaining to him how or why his disobedience makes you crazy or is unacceptable, will do little or nothing to change or guide his behavior. Your immediate movement to action (or a consequence, like the loss of a story at bedtime) will teach him that obedience is mandatory. You are making a request for a reason (which you may or may not choose to tell him), and his job is to comply. The boundary lines are laid, and the child knows that to "be good" in your home means he will answer with compliance when you speak.

If you're not quite sold on the idea yet that being the boss is one of the primary means of raising kids that are compliant, let me give you one more scenario, where Pookie is now 16:

Mommy: "Where are you going, Pookie?"

Pookie: "Out." (picking up mommy's car keys)

Mommy: "With who? And Pookie, you can't take my car, I need it to pick up your brother from practice...."

Pookie: "I'm going out with friends. I'll be back later. My bro can get a ride home from someone else."

Mommy: "Oh, OK.... Don't be too late, k?"

Don't think it's an exaggeration. It will go down this way (or similarly) if you don't take charge of your 2 year old. Or worse, if you decide when he's a teenager that it's essential that he's compliant, Pookie will vehemently disagree, and battles, screaming matches, and constant power struggles will erupt. Even if your child is not blatantly rebellious in his teenage years, he will defy you or resent you then if you don't diligently teach him to respect you now.

So who's going to be the boss of your house? (I say that with a wink and a nudge, I already know the answer!)

CHAPTER 2

House Rules

A few years back (okay, maybe going on a decade now), I was involved in a brilliant group called MOPS, or Mothers of Preschoolers. It was an opportunity to sit down (shocking) once a week, with food not prepared by me (hallelujah!), listen to someone teach me *without* my children by my side (SOLD!), and spend some much-needed time with grown-ups. Most of the ladies were around my age, rearing their little ankle biters just like me. But there were also a handful of "older and wiser" women who were there to encourage, guide, teach, and mentor us.

One of those women, who incidentally raised and

homeschooled 5 children (my hat is *off* to that woman!) shared with us that their family had two House Rules. They were simple: Be Kind, and Listen & Obey. I loved them. After listening to four years of whining, feet-dragging, stomping, moaning, and more whining from my brood, we added a third to the list: No Grumbling or Complaining. We now had 3 House Rules that have endured to this day, and which, amazingly, seem to cover almost every infraction the kids have conjured up. The house rules, incidentally, also help our family to define what it means to "Be Good".

Rule #1: Be Kind

This one is pretty straightforward, and we use the Golden Rule to define it more clearly for them: Treat others the way you want to be treated. If you don't want someone grabbing your toys, then don't grab theirs. If you don't want others hitting you, then don't hit them. If you enjoy being treated respectfully, then treat others with respect. I love this rule because it's pretty easy to make a quick comparison for them to get them to see when they've broken it. "Do you want someone else using your toothbrush to clean their Legos? No, you think that's disgusting? Then don't use his!" Point taken.

Rule #2: Listen and Obey

We expect the kids in our house to comply with our requests, and to do it promptly. Our goal is "first time obedience", meaning *I ask you to do something, you do it*. However, they often get distracted, are doing something that diverts their attention, or are just plain being lazy at the moment, and so I'll give a warning and a proposed consequence right then if follow through doesn't happen right away. For example, I might say "Child, put your shoes on please and get your back-pack ready for school." (No movement in that direction). "Child, if you don't do what I've asked now, that cookie I planned to give you for snack at school is staying here." (Child moves to comply. Imagine that.)

Rule #3: No Grumbling or Complaining

This one encompasses anything that denotes irritation, hesitation, or unhappiness at following the other 2 rules, or anything else that's going down (like the vegetable beef stew I made for dinner). You know that sound that kids make when they don't want to do something? I don't know if the English language will allow me to write it, but it sounds something like, "AWWWwwwWWW!!" Do you know what I'm talking about? If you've heard it once or twice or 12,326 times, you know what I mean. In our house, straight up complaining is prohibited, but even that *sound* is unacceptable. It implies a sense of irritation at being "put out" by our requests that simply does not make for a peaceful, enjoyable household.

I like to tell my kids this little "parable" of sorts to remind them of *why* that sound, those complaints, and that grumbling, is unacceptable.

The "THERE IS NO GRUMBLING IN THIS HOUSEHOLD" parable:

There once was a mother who had a gaggle of children. And she had a LOT of laundry to do, a LOT of dishes to do, a LOT of cooking to do, and a LOT of cleaning to do. All the time. Every day. Every night. Cleaning, folding clothes, putting stuff away, scrubbing nasty peed-on toilets, cooking endless meals, washing mounds of pots, pans and sippy cups, mopping spills on floors. The cycle was endless. She did not love doing all of these chores, and yet she did not complain to her children about it, and they always had clean clothes to wear, healthy food to eat, a tidy-ish house, and toilets that usually didn't reek of pee. And again, although she DID NOT LOVE the chores, she DID NOT COMPLAIN.

The End.

Grumbling gives the sense that the requests being made are annoying at best and unreasonable at worst.

I also like to remind my kids that there are children who awaken before dawn and take care of the animals on their farm for 2 hours, head off to school all day, then resume farm duties as soon as they get home until dark (I do not know these children, but I have heard that they exist.). This is a reminder that unloading 1/3 of the dishwasher is NOT an unreasonable request, as they are a part of this household and enjoy the benefits of clean dishes and the food that was on them, multiple times a day. Do you need to hear my parable again, child?

Not allowing grumbling also has the benefit of encouraging one of my favorite virtues: *Gratitude*. When we grumble about what's not so good, we're not counting our blessings. When a grumble erupts (or even a pouty face), we talk about what we're thankful for, reminding us that there's almost always more good than bad in our little Wells world.

These three House Rules have set up a definitive boundary in our household, or if you're visual, picture a "pathway", of acceptable behavior. When the kids veer off the path, there are consequences that encourage, pull, prod, lure, or sometimes even yank them back onto the path, depending on how far, how defiantly, or how dangerously they've stepped off.

For example, if the kids are outside playing and a loud, angry (irritating) argument breaks out (shocking, I know) over a game, I call both kids in and this is a common conversation:

Mommy: "What happened, Child #1?"

Child #1: "He changed the rules in the middle of the game!!"

Mommy: "Did you feel frustrated by that?"

Child #1: "YES!!!"

Mommy: "Did you react to him with kindness, or were you rude?"

Child #2: "I was rude."

Mommy: "What did you see happen, Child #2?"

Child #2: "I changed the rules because no one was following the rules anyway!!"

Mommy: "And how would you feel if someone changed the rules in the middle of a game and you didn't have a say in it?"

Child #2: "Bad. Frustrated."

Mommy: "So did you treat him the way you would want to be treated?"

Child #2: "No."

Mommy: "What rule did you break, Children?"

Both children: "Be Kind."

Mommy: "Both of you go stand in the corner and think about what you could have done differently."

A few minutes later I pull them out, and have them look at each other. Immediately now (because they know the drill) they apologize, and most of the time they *mean it*. They both know they broke a House Rule, and they both know they need to (or at least are going to) be held accountable. They're learning to recognize that *even when others do maddening, frustrating, irritating things, the only thing they can control is themselves and their own reactions.*

They alone are responsible for their behavior, and they will be held accountable if a House Rule is broken. The path is clear, they know when they've stepped off of it, and they accept that it's my job to correct the miss-step.

We give our kids a gift when we give them the tools they need to manage their own behavior, to have the self-discipline to react in ways that are counter-intuitive to human nature (selfish human nature tells them "I want it my way, and I want it *now!*"). We are not wild animals, I like to remind my kids. We are intelligent humans who have the power to make decisions to *act* in ways we don't *feel like* acting.

I don't usually "feel like" being patient when they are acting like little demanding tyrants, or insulting one another, or in any other way breaking the House Rules. Trust me, I have to muster every ounce of my patience and energy at times to keep from becoming the "Scary Guy" I mentioned earlier (and I certainly fail to keep myself in check sometimes too – I am half Italian after all.)

However, when I fail, I have learned to quickly acknowledge my wrongdoing and apologize, whether for losing my cool, raising my voice, or being overly-harsh if that was the case. I don't try to "take it back", but I *do* take responsibility for my approach or tone. I might say, "What you did was not OK, but my response in being rude/loud/angry wasn't OK either. Please forgive me for losing my temper."

However, I know that if I keep my cool and follow through, I'm:

1. Setting an example for them to follow (more on this in the next chapter);

2. Giving them tools to learn self-discipline and responsibility for their own actions;

3. Helping to create a more peaceful atmosphere in our home where they feel safe, and where others feel welcome and *want* to hang out.

I've explained to my kids on plenty of occasions that when they insult, injure, threaten, or disrespect another one of my children, it's my job to protect my (other) child. Our home is a safe place to be, and it's the job of the parents to ensure that everyone feels safe. How safe does a child feel if his sibling is allowed to hit him, demean him, call him names, disrespect him, or in any other way emotionally or physically abuse him? It only took one time for my oldest son to hit his younger brother (he was itty bitty at the time) for me to recognize that this was *unacceptable* in our home. Momma Bear came out to defend her youngest child. Momma Bear continues to protect her kids, oftentimes from one another!

Our children know that we will keep each of them safe, others both inside and outside of our home will be respected and treated with kindness, and we will not grumble and act as if life has somehow been "unfair" to us. Our house rules ensure that we are pressing on toward those goals.

And a little side-note on "fair". If we had a 4th rule it would be this (and I've said it a million times if I've said it once): **We don't talk about fair.** Life is not fair, it never has been and never will be, and I will not be responsible for trying to make it that way when it's not. Another way I explain that to them is, "different kids get different things at different times." It does no service to kids to attempt to "even the score" at all times, when Life will not do that for them, EVER. So just the word "fair" begins a long monologue from this Mommy that my kids have learned to avoid. We just don't talk about fair.

CHAPTER 3

Monkey See, Monkey Do

From the time they're tiny, Little Ones begin parroting what we say. That driver who cut me off (and formerly I might have called a not-so-nice-name!) is now a "crazy guy", and the stupid computer is being "silly" when it freezes on me – lest my kids repeat the inappropriate words that I'm tempted to say. And I cannot be hypocritical and expect them NOT to do the very things I'm doing. "Mom, why can't I have chocolate for breakfast? You are!" (That's why I hide out in my bedroom when I'm having chocolate for breakfast.)

If I want my kids to be polite, then barking at them, "GO PICK UP YOUR TOYS, THIS HOUSE IS A MESS AND

WE'RE LEAVING IN 10 MINUTES! YOU'RE MAKING ME CRAZY!!" is teaching them that it's appropriate to be loud and rude when I want something done or am feeling pressed for time. And I can rest assured they will use that same approach when the time comes. "Can you please pick up your toys? We're leaving in 10 minutes" produces the same result *if I'm consistent in having them follow through on the request.* I can see you raising an eyebrow. I'm serious.

My husband and I have had a few (a-hem) disagreements over this through the years. He's prone, at times, to barking orders, coming from a line of work where it's imperative that what is "requested" *happens now.* (He's a Battalian Chief with the fire department). On the homefront, though, it's a different story. We are not training fire-fighters (yet), we are training children who we want to grow into happy, respectable, responsible adults.

We both agree that when we ask for something from our kids, it needs to happen, and it needs to happen promptly. But our approach to our requests has much to teach them too. "Sweetheart, can you clean up the family room before we leave? I don't like leaving the house a mess!" tells them the same thing as "I HAVE TOLD YOU A MILLION TIMES WE'RE NOT LEAVING UNTIL THIS ROOM IS CLEAN!!! YOU ARE DRIVING ME NUTS!!" But, I'm giving my child an example of calmly (but firmly) presenting expectations to him, explaining my reasoning, and giving him a chance to learn those skills and use them in the future, if I choose the first approach.

Believe me, though, when I say that I'm holding my tongue – I AM frustrated from asking it for the gazillionth time this week! And I do fall short far too often and explode – both the kids and my husband will attest to that.

When one of my children is frustrated with his sibling (did you know kids tend to get annoyed with their brothers and sisters from time to time?) he has a choice of shouting, "LEAVE ME ALONE, BOOGER-FACE!!!" (which he'll get busted for) or he can choose to calmly say, "Can you stop bugging me? I want to be left alone right now". Incidentally, it's also my job to ensure that his sibling honors that request as it was presented so appropriately and respectfully. (See House Rules #1 and #2.)

Remember that Authoritarian parenting (dictator-ish) style we talked about? Here's the example she's setting, and how it might go down:

Mommy: "POOKIE, GET THAT SIPPY CUP OFF THE COUCH NOW! I HAVE TOLD YOU A MILLION TIMES TO KEEP YOUR SIPPY CUPS ON THE TABLE!! LOOK AT THE MESS YOU'VE MADE!!! WHY ARE YOU SO NAUGHTY? GO TO YOUR ROOM, YOU'RE KILLING ME!"

(Later that day...)

Pookie: (Grabbing a toy back from his little sister) "SISTER, I HAVE TOLD YOU A MILLION TIMES NOT TO TAKE MY TOYS!!! YOU'RE SO NAUGHTY, YOU'RE KILLING ME!!"

Think how confused Pookie will be when he's told not to talk to his sister that way – "If Mommy does it, why can't I?" The double standard is creating a state of confusion and unclear boundaries in their household, and the lesson is, "do as I say, not as I do." But the problem is, then what *is* Pookie to do, if it's not what

Mommy is doing? He is counting on her to show him how to be good, yet she herself is not demonstrating it.

It's imperative that we as the parent set the example in our home of what "good" behavior looks like. We are the adults, and we have the high calling of setting the emotional climate in our household, meaning we are not going to be driven by the emotional outbursts or irritating behaviors of our kids. In fact, we even have the high calling of *turning the tide* when emotions (tantrums, whining, arguing) are flying high!

Did you know we are wired for happiness (or grumpiness) from a very early age? Along with our given temperaments and our genetic make-up, we have neuronal pathways that are being forged beginning when we're infants for joyfulness, crabbiness and all the emotions in between.

Per the documentary *Happy*, our experiences, both profound ones and little day-to-day ones, help us to develop either common or rare opportunities for future joyfulness. Specifically, the neurotransmitter dopamine (one of the "happy hormone") seems to have a "use it or lose it" effect on the brain. Thus, as we experience happiness, it appears that using those happy neurotransmitters actually encourages more dopamine to be produced, more receptors to develop, and thus more opportunities for future happiness! (One of the primary ways to drum up dopamine seems to be spending time in community - like with others who offer us *love, acceptance and belonging* – there's those 3 gifts again!). It also appears happiness is contagious: *"The more you have, the more everyone has!"* (Roko Belic, 2011).

Have you ever known a family that loves to laugh? They seem to laugh over everything: They laugh at commercials on TV, they laugh at themselves and each other (and it seems like everyone laughs along instead of getting defensive or having their feelings hurt.) They laugh over stubbed toes, spilled milk, and crazy hair days – and it's a joy to be around them! Guess what? They are practicing joyfulness, and the more they practice it, the easier it is for them to "pull up" that joy in the future. Those neuronal pathways for happiness, and the neurotransmitters (dopamine, serotonin, etc.) that are being produced get easier to produce the more they occur when we're young. So what are we getting at?

Set an example of happiness, joyfulness, playfulness, fun-lovingness, light-heartedness, politeness, kindness, calmness, respectfulness, and patience to your kids whenever possible (use coffee, if necessary). Our example sets a stage for them to experience even more of those feelings for the rest of their lives!

CHAPTER 4

Call In The Reinforcements

So a long time ago (remember, I'm no scholar, just a college grad and mommy), there was a behavior researcher named Pavlov. He was a cool dude I'm sure, because he loved dogs and dogs are amazing (I'm ad-libbing that part, assuming it's true because he did a lot of his studies on them). Anyway, he discovered what most of us instinctively know and can observe in the real world: Dogs (and people) respond to rewards.

Pavlov discovered that his dogs would begin to salivate just at the arrival of his assistants in a room, as those assistants brought them food.

Following Pavlov's discovery, another behaviorist,

B.F. Skinner discovered something similar but even more remarkable: Mice would quickly learn to press a lever if it meant food was dispensed when they did it (McLeod, 2007).

So how does this relate to our little offspring that we're so desperately trying to teach "good behavior" to? It's pretty simple: *Humans also respond to rewards.* (Shocking, right?)

"Suzie, if you put on your shoes and tidy up your room, we'll go get an ice cream cone!"

"Johnny, if you get your homework done quickly and neatly, we'll have time to go out for pizza tonight!"

You can bet Suzie's shoes are on and her room was cleaned up in record time, and Johnny's homework was done neatly and accurately at super-speed that night.

Interestingly, though, most of the time the reward doesn't have to be so ambitious. Ice cream and pizza nights cost money and take time that we don't always have. But many rewards are simple, take little or no time, and are free. For example, "Great job on getting your room picked up! Now you can go outside and play!" FREE (and buys you time alone in the house to sip some coffee and leisurely fold your 5th load of laundry for the day).

> "Thanks for being so helpful with your sister so I can start dinner!"

> "You did a great job on that homework, buddy! I'm so proud of how neat your handwriting is!"

> "You put your shoes on by yourself, what a big girl!"

> "I can't believe you're already big enough to clean up your blocks all by yourself! I'm so proud of you!"

These rewards (simple compliments and encouragement) can often be enough "pre-motivation" to get your Pookie helping, home-working, putting on shoes alone, and block-picking-upping next time (or maybe, more realistically, after a few encouraging compliments from you) without any prompting. Can you imagine?

We also use a marble system of rewards that over the years has evolved to fit the growing and changing needs of our family. It's simple, easy to follow through on, and when used consistently, works to encourage our kids to behave with kindness, and complete their responsibilities (chores), with a good attitude.

Here's how it works: We have a bowl full of marbles, and 4 glass jars next to it, each holding a popsicle stick with each child's name on it. Throughout the day, our kids receive a marble or two for good behavior (they put it in the jar themselves), especially for the things that are most important to us. Marbles are only given at my direction, so if someone asks for a marble, the answer is always, "that's up to me, I'll let you know if you've earned one!"

If someone shares without being asked, is particularly helpful, moves to action when directed promptly and without grumbling, picks up toys or cleans their room without being asked, a marble is earned. At the end of each day, 3 more marbles are given if all their typical daily chores have been done too.

They can also lose marbles for unkind behavior, for failing to follow through on a given request, or for any deliberate disobedience. (This is called "negative reinforcement", more coming on this later in this chapter and the next).

After 50 marbles, a reward is earned. When they were little, it earned them a simple $5 max "date" with mom or dad, like an ice cream cone or a trip to Toys R Us for a Lego Minifigure or the Dollar Tree. As the kids have grown, 50 marbles is now worth $10 cash for the kids 10 and over, and has become their way of earning allowance. The youngest earns the TV show of her choice for 50 marbles, her favorite reward. This method works well for our family and other families I know who've tried it, because:

1. Just dropping a marble in the jar is reinforcing (even the sound of it clinking to a Little One is a reward in itself!)

2. It's a simple way to quickly reward good behaviors.

3. As far as negative reinforcement goes, removing a marble is quick and helps a crazed parent move to swift action when a rule is broken.

4. We're not over-doing it on the reward (it typically takes 3 -4 weeks or so to earn 50 marbles).

When a reward is too high, the child begins to expect overly-ambitious prizes for simple, expected behaviors, and it becomes increasingly difficult to find effective rewards. This is why we love the marble system! A marble or two is quick and relatively cheap (worth between 10-20 cents each, depending on your reward after 50), and doesn't create a need in the child to get something every time he complies. In fact, we deliberately only offer marbles every so often (this is called intermittent reinforcement), and not every time a good deed is done, so that the marbles don't become expected *or* lose their value to the child.

A famous behavioral psychologist, B.F. Skinner, discovered the theory of "intermittent reinforcement". It's the idea that rewards that are offered only every so often produce the "desired" behavior to be performed more frequently. This is because, a.) the uncertainty of a reward makes the hope that it might happen increase the frequency of a desired behavior, and b.) anything given too often loses it's desirability (imagine eating a cookie all day long after every task you completed. Would you really still want another cookie as a reward at the end of the day?) (Macleod, 2007).

Positive reinforcements are powerful tools for modifying behaviors. In fact, in a daily training context, positive reinforcements are best at changing behaviors in the long-term, as they establish in the person (child) both a joy for and a longing to perform well in the future, which means less negative or unwanted behaviors, and more positive, desirable behaviors. It also means less yelling, nagging, disciplining, complaining, arguing, and tantruming (you, not them) for the family.

Negative reinforcement is the opposite effect, where a person will discontinue a behavior if a negative outcome occurs. For example, if I get burned by the oven every time I open it and put my hand inside without an oven mitt, I will learn pretty quickly to wear a mitt. If Johnny steps on a thorn every time he leaves the house without putting his shoes on, he will quickly learn to put his shoes on first.

Negative reinforcements work. Kind of like salt in a cookie recipe, though, use just the right amount and it improves the cookie. Use too much and you want to wretch when you eat them. Negative reinforcements should be reserved for the times when you missed the opportunity to meet them at the pass with something encouraging, or you truly need to discontinue a disobedient or dangerous behavior.

Here's a scenario where the negative reinforcement is instilled by the parent:

> Mommy: "Sugar Bear, do not throw that toy." (toward your baby brother's head – SCARY.)
>
> Sugar bear throws the toy.
>
> Mommy: "No, DANGER!"
>
> Mommy immediately moves Sugar Bear into her bed for a time out (protecting baby brother in the process, and hopefully in the future as well).

A few months ago during a lunar eclipse, we learned that a neighbor down the street had a huge telescope we could look in to see the eclipse up close. The kids and I took off running down the street to catch a glimpse before the eclipse passed. The oldest said he wasn't coming, but changed his mind after we left, and set off after us (in the dark) at break-neck speed on his skateboard. He hit a crack in the sidewalk and took a painful spill, and ended up with scrapes and bruises that took weeks to heal. He got up from the crash and said, "I'm never riding my skateboard again!!" to which I answered, "well, probably not in the dark, anyway!" He experienced a natural negative consequence for a (mildly un-wise) choice he had made. And he's still convinced he'll never night-time skateboard again.

In this next chapter will go more in-depth into when and how to apply age-appropriate negative reinforcements. Sometimes they're the only effective tools we have when those not-so-good behaviors crop up.

CHAPTER 5

Crimes & Punishments
(A.K.A. Behavior Modification 101)

In a perfect world we would offer so much constructive guidance and balanced praise that our kids would naturally know how to Be Good. But in the real world, kids (all people, really) do undesirable things, and boundaries need to be set. Disciplining our children gives us the ability to herd our Little Ones back onto the path of appropriate behaviors when they've stepped out of line.

We must always remember, though, that our kids are a work in progress. They don't automatically know what's "good", and it's our job to make sure they're crystal clear on what's expected of them. Getting irritated that they're not "obeying" or following the rules when the rules were never clearly laid out for them sets them up for failure.

Set them up for success by making expectations crystal clear, using respectful tones and language to communicate them. Firmly but lovingly remind them when they're breaking (or look like they're about to break) a rule. But if they choose the infraction, it's time to take swift action to correct it, and prevent it from becoming a habit or lead them to believe it's ok "just this once".

We've all heard it said, "let the punishment fit the crime." Although theoretically we know, to some extent, that this works, sometimes it's hard to know how to find a consequence that fits each crime (and there's no shortage of childish "crimes" to be committed!). So we'll move back into one of my favorite areas, psychology, to understand what works to change and mold behaviors to get the desired result: Rewards and punishments.

When babies are little, rewards start coming early:

Sucking produces milk. Smiling produces coos and smiles back. Crying means soothing is coming (and eventually, if it doesn't, the crying will often stop).

As they grow into bouncing baby-hood, they're rewarded for sitting with claps and cheers. Eating their veggies means smiles and "what a good eater you are!" Then crawling, standing, and walking, gets even more happy faces, giggles, and encouragement from mommy and daddy. For most parents, these types of rewards come naturally and instinctively.

As the baby gets a bit older, though, negative behaviors begin to emerge as well. Baby doesn't want a di-dee change, so he tries to kick or even roll off the changing table. He doesn't like mushy spinach and spits it out. He grabs mommy's hair and pulls when she's holding him. He fights going into the car seat by arching his back and fussing, maybe even taking a swing to whap the face in front of him. What's a parent to do? The sweet, innocent baby is getting a mind of his own, and it's getting harder to manage him!

By 9 - 12 months, babies have developed more learned behaviors, and the strictly instinctual behaviors of infancy begin to fade. He's beginning to realize that his actions produce *re*-actions (some desirable, some not so desirable), and it's the perfect time to start training.

When he grabs mommy's hair while she's carrying him or putting him in the car seat, she can hold his little hand and firmly say, "No! That hurts mommy!" If or when he tries it again, it's Time Out time. When he kicks or fights during a diaper change, holding his two feet firmly in one hand while continuing the diaper change might work, while saying "lay nicely, please!". Feistier babies may try to squirm or roll their way off the changing table, which might warrant a little smack to the back of the leg (don't judge me! It's my job to protect my baby from harm, and halting this unsafe behavior is the goal). He needs to understand in no uncertain terms that I am the boss (for his good!), and his behavior is unacceptable and even dangerous. (Not only does squirming smear poop all over his clothes and the changing table, he could fall and really hurt himself!).

When he spits out his spinach, you have two choices: Remove him from his high chair and put him in his crib for a minute (and say "no spitting!" as you set him down), or just say "no, no!" with firmness and a little squeeze to his cheeks, not to cause him pain but to equate the "no" with the spitting (some babies will respond quickly just to the tone). But ignoring it will only reward the behavior, and he'll learn that when he doesn't want something, spitting is an acceptable response. In our house, spitting is not acceptable. It's messy, yucky, and rude.

Time out is what psychologists call "response cost". When Little One does something undesirable, there will be an undesirable consequence. When they're still itty bitty (9 months to around 2 years), time out in the crib is ideal. Baby is contained and safe, and removed from the positive reinforcement of being with the people and things he loves. (And no, it will not cause him to equate his bed with negativity. Children are extremely perceptive, and the calm, soothing naptime and bedtime routines will look nothing like the firm placement of baby into a bed with "time out, no hitting mommy!" from you. He will definitively know the difference.) Make sure paci, blankey or any other soothers are not in the bed when you leave him there. The point is for him to feel uncomfortable for a bit.

After age 2, a time out corner or chair works great, especially when it's out of sight of the happy goings-on of the rest of the household. It's essential to train them from the get-go, though, that they are not to get up or out of that spot until you (the Boss) have determined that it's time. Start by keeping the chair close to you initially and firmly setting him back there if he gets up – most children will try that at least once before they "get it". And notice that I said firmly, not roughly. Go for calm and controlled placement.

Once they get that you mean business, you can move the chair a little further from the hub of the house, so they're not getting the satisfaction of being amused by what's going on while they sit. A general rule of thumb is to have them stay in time out for the number of minutes corresponding to their age (2 years old, 2 minute time out). Training your Little One to stay in time out early on is key. He has the job of learning a new behavior during that time, but my job of running a household continues, so going back to the dishes, cooking, folding, or whatever I was working on, while that time passes, is ideal.

To spank or not to spank

OK, friend, keep an open mind here. I realize this is a "hot button" topic for many. But before you throw the book (or device you're reading it on) in the trash, hear me out on how and why I believe in *very limited* spankings, and you can decide if it's harsh, mean or abusive (words I've heard from many parents who disagree with its use). Also know that I'm not trying to convince you of its merits, but rather explain how and why it can be useful, and share one of the methods we used in parenting our Little Ones that worked to instill respect and obedience, especially when the stakes were high.

First and foremost, spanking is not the same as hitting. If I wound up and smacked my kid every time he did something unacceptable, I would rightfully be labeled abusive. I do not use my hands to react in anger to the behavior of my children. That's not spanking, it's retaliation and it results in fearful and/or rebellious kids. This is certainly not the goal or intention.

Spanking in our family is reserved for 3 infractions: Truly dangerous behaviors (like running in the street after being told not to, hitting another person, throwing objects in anger toward another, or pushing another from the top of the slide, etc.), deliberately lying (we need to be able to trust our kids implicitly), and intentional disrespect or disobedience (like hitting an adult or saying "NO!" to a request from a parent or elder). Whether you believe me or not, spanking is rarely used in families where it's being used appropriately. It's rare for 2 reasons:

1.) The infraction must be great and must fall into one of the above categories.
2.) Once the child has been spanked properly for an infraction, it's unlikely to happen a second time.

Let me give you an example. Like all responsible parents, when he was tiny, I told my oldest son to stay out of the street, and held his hand whenever we got near the edge of the street to keep him safe. I would also point to the street and say "danger!" if he ever attempted to step into it without holding my hand.

By the time he was 3, he knew that the street was strictly off-limits for him when he wasn't with an adult. So when at age 3 (he had a little 1 ½ year old brother watching too) he ran into the street after a ball, I knew that the best option for halting that behavior pronto was a spanking. I ran (frantically) and got him from the street, took him firmly (not roughly) in to his room, and told him yet again how dangerous the street is. I explained that listening to mommy keeps him safe, and when he disobeys and endangers himself he needs a spanking so he won't do it again. I used a wooden spoon (the same implement my own parents used – to avoid using a hand and the child ever equating your hand to pain), and he got 3 swift swats on the behind with the spoon. He cried, and I cried. But he never ran in the street again (EVER!), and I could trust him from there on out whenever we were near a street's edge.

If this sounds like abuse to you, then don't do it! If your parents or another adult was overly harsh or physical with you, I can only imagine that you shudder at this method. There are other negative reinforcements that will work effectively to re-direct behavior.

However, I've also learned from experience that when a child's behavior is extreme enough, and the benefits of a quick and effective lesson is necessary (as in the case of keeping a child safe), spanking works.

I also believe, as I've said previously, that it's my job to keep my *other* children from harm, and provide a loving, safe environment for everyone in our home, so when one child is hurting, pushing, biting, throwing at, or in any other way being abusive toward another child, it's my responsibility to *stop that behavior.*

When little Wells Boy #3 arrived, he came into a household with 2 big brothers: A barely 3-year old, and a 21-month old (rather impulsive and self-focused ages, right?). So when his "big" 21-month old brother thought throwing a toy Thomas train at his infant brother's head was a good way to get mommy's attention, mommy stepped in quickly to protect the tiniest one from damage. After a talk about "danger", and a spanking, we could rest assured Brother #2 never threw anything at his baby again. (In fact, he became one of his greatest protectors and defenders in the months to come!)

Although time-out can be highly effective at stopping a child from hitting another, it may take multiple lessons to train that out of the child as the "reward" of watching another child cry or react to pain is often higher than the consequence of a time out. I never had to worry that our 3 boys (20 and 21 months between them) would hit or hurt each other, because we trained them from the get-go that this was entirely unacceptable, and we would be swiftly stopping any behaviors that put another person in danger.

I remember a time many years ago being told by a friend that she doesn't believe "hitting a child is a good way to teach them not to hit." After she left, I asked my boys (at that time they were about 7, 5 and 4) if I had ever hit them. They looked at me shocked and said, "no!!". Yet all of them had been spanked for one infraction or another at that point.

Once again, children are highly perceptive and know the difference between someone hitting another person in frustration or anger, and a parent's response of stopping dangerous or defiant behavior with appropriate and wisely-administered consequences.

Other Appropriate Discipline

We've already talked a bit about time-out, a tried-and-true method of stopping unwanted behavior. As our kids got older (and bigger, smarter, and sassier), time-out happened in a corner. Around age 7, a chair didn't work as well as it used to because they could always find something to amuse themselves with while sitting there. So my brilliant (and obedience-focused) husband started using a corner as their "thinking space", like his parents did when whenever he misbehaved as a child. They stood with their nose in the corner until told to come out.

Sounds a bit uncomfortable perhaps, but realize that by the time the child was 7, the rule he had broken had been broken no less that 1,826 times (and that's being generous), and the child knew he was breaking that rule *again*. The point is this: Children at this age should know what is expected of them, the path has been clearly laid (for a number of years), so their breaking of the rule justifiably needs a stronger correction to prevent its recurrence.

Other options include taking away a revered item. Here's another scenario (tell me if you're shocked by it because it would *never* happen in your home):

Child #1: "That's MY toy, give it back!!! Mommy, he took my toy! I set it down for just a second and he STOLE IT!"

Child #2: "You weren't playing with it! You left to play with the other toy!"

Child #1: "I was coming back, and besides it's MINE!!! Mommy, tell him to give it back!!"

Mommy: "Children, why do we have toys?"

Children: "To have fun and share."

Mommy: "Is fighting over them fun, or is sharing them more fun?"

Children: "Sharing is more fun."

Mommy: "Give me the toy, it's mine for today."

Back to punishments fitting crimes, taking an item away when it's being mis-used, causing conflict, or hasn't been authorized to be played with is an appropriate and natural consequence. And, in the above scenario, the added benefit is that it quickly ends the argument and re-establishes the peace. It also encourages them to work out their issues apart from me playing "middle man", as my involvement usually means the loss of something for both of them.

When my son was 2, I remember lamenting to my sister-in-law that I felt like all I ever did was say "no". The mainstay of my parenting seemed to be training out undesirable behaviors. It can be an exhausting, seemingly endless and arduous task. But during the early years, firm and consistent training means by age 3 or 4, our kids are becoming more compliant and stepping off the "path" a lot less frequently. The boundaries have been laid, and the encouragement to "be good" has been established. Rules and expectations have been clearly laid out, and for the most part the Little One knows what to do and what *not* do. And you'll find that you – and others – are having more opportunities to enjoy your time with him. He's respectful, well-mannered, compliant, and (although certainly still feisty and strong-willed at times – aren't we all?!) pretty fun to be around!

CHAPTER 6

A United Front
(Subtitle: Just Do It)

For families with both parents at home, this chapter is an imperative element to raising those "good" kids we're all hoping and praying for, so after you read this, hand it over to your spouse for a glance at it too (don't worry, husband, you'll get on board with it pretty quickly, especially the second half. Come on, it's called "Just Do It". And I'm not talking about discipline here.)

All parents enter into parenting with their own pre-conceived ideas about what it entails. We know what kind of parent we plan to be (no one intends to be a big pushover whose kids walk all over them, right? Or a screaming tyrant the neighbor kids are afraid of?), but experiences from our own upbringing typically shape the methods we'll choose and how we *in actuality* will perform. Most of us hope we're going to win Parent of the Year, and correct all the mistakes our parents made, as we raise up our Perfect Brood. Most of us are sorely mistaken, unless we make a concerted effort to redirect ourselves, and trust that as we make mistakes (and I've made plenty of them!), we will also learn from them along the way.

When it comes to discipline, kids have a pretty keen sense early on what type of parents they're dealing with. They can also sniff out the "weak link" the way we can sniff out a dirty di-dee. There ain't no mistaking which parent will cave when Shnookums wants her way. Even babies will crawl toward the parent that will give them the attention, affection, play, toys, food, etc. that they desire (which is why mommy is often the preferred parent for tiny babies: She wears the positive reinforcement on her chest, or if not nursing, is often the primary giver of the bottle – and food is a powerful reinforcer.)

The point is this: If one parent is attempting to "train" consistently, reinforce good behaviors and discourage undesirable behaviors (hopefully in a respectful, loving way), and yet the other parent is undermining, questioning, challenging or disagreeing with that parent's methods, little Shnookums is going to start pushing her boundaries with the "easy" parent early on. And Schnookums will watch with satisfaction as discord ensues between the parents (and the attention is diverted from her bad behavior in the process. She's no dummy).

Our goal as parents is not just to instill good behavior in our precious offspring. The primary intention should be to create a sanctuary for our families (and others who come over). *Peace and harmony* is the goal for the household. This means that parents need to support one another, once a parenting decision has been made, that allows the child to see unity between them. Hear this (and it's hard, almost painful at times): *Even if you vehemently disagree with how the other parent has chosen to respond to the child in the current moment, save your concern for later (even 3 minutes later in the other room!).* Kids thrive in an environment where they know mommy has daddy's back, and daddy will support mommy's decisions.

We've all seem families where the parents can't find the happy meeting point between them, and there's constant discord. Of course, kids typically tend toward the "permissive" behavioral control (or lack of) of the lax parent, even when the other may be trying to instill appropriate and healthy boundaries. Here's how to determine if you might be a permissive parent:

1. Do you think or say, "Kids will be kids!" when your child does something rude, annoying or disobedient?
2. Do you put your child's desire for "happiness" before your own (or others) wants/needs (even if it's for peace and quiet)?
3. Do you think your child is the cutest/smartest/most amazing creature on the planet, and really can do no wrong?

Every child is amazing. Every child is precious beyond imagine. Every child ought to be nurtured, encouraged, and loved unconditionally. Every child also deserves to be trained, guided, and corralled toward appropriate behavior. And remember, the rest of the world does not appreciate the "adorable" tantrum your child is having in the grocery store or in Starbucks. Certainly not at dinner in a restaurant.

If your other half is attempting to teach your kiddos to "be good", but you think it's just too many boundaries, or too much discipline, think to yourself: What do I want my kids to carry into adulthood? I'm hopeful your answers might be something like:

1. Learn how to be responsible.
2. Learn how to respect himself & others.
3. Learn how to care for himself & his environment.
4. Learn how to be a "good citizen", making his world (or even block or household) a better place.
5. Learn how to respect authority.

If these are the goals you're striving toward for the future, you have to start while they're tiny. Good behavior is caught, taught, and trained most easily early on in life. So, easy-going parent, get on board with the more structured, boundary-setting parent. Boundary-setting parent, be sensitive and respectful with how you ask your more lax partner, to come alongside you.

And both of you, don't challenge your spouse's choice in his discipline approach (or lack there-of) in front of the kids! Just DON'T DO IT.

Ok, that leads us to the next point. Parents, seriously, your marriage is of utmost, primary importance to your kids. The security, safety, and confidence that a stable marriage brings to a family is paramount. And remember: Your behavior toward one another is setting an example to your kids on how to behave, both toward you and especially toward others (friends and siblings), as they will transfer your relationship methods to their siblings and peers.

Prioritize your marriage. OK (men, you're gonna like me for this): Prioritize your "bedroom activities". Even when life is crazy, when sleep is at a premium, when the kids have sucked, zapped, and stolen every ounce of your energy and zeal, there's still time for it. I'm NOT KIDDING.

Being intimate doesn't have to be a major event. Think about it, we don't dread a quick hug, we don't put off a simple, sweet kiss (especially from our Little Ones!), so why do we think being intimate has to be a major, energy-sapping marathon when we don't even have time to take a shower or even use the bathroom (alone) half of the time? This is a simple way to physically and emotionally re-connect with each other when all the other ways we used to connect (dates, walks, conversations of any sort) have gone by the baby-takes-over wayside.

I say this because I have met so many couples over the years who have let their bedroom activities "dip" (sometimes into non-existence) after baby arrives. And in the wake of the "dip" is typically at least one partner feeling neglected or disconnected. And there's such a simple solution!

There's a famous company who had the primary market on athletic equipment for a while there, and if I'm correct they're still doing OK. Part of it may be their amazingly simple yet profound marketing. (Someone better be a gazillionaire by now for thinking it up, because it's been used and way over-used, including in this little book you're now reading, for a long time). And for good reason. It speaks volumes with just 3 little words, and you may find your marriage regain a spark, and find your spouse a little (or even a lot) more agreeable, by following its wisdom: Just do it!

CHAPTER 7

R&R

Although most of us interpret "R&R" as rest and relaxation, for our purposes we're going to use a similar but possibly more relevant descriptive for what parents truly need: recharge and reboot.

Built in to every day there needs to be some downtime for parents. I know that sounds nearly impossible and maybe even laughable, but early on, R&R can happen (even for 15 minutes!) during naptime for baby. As your Little One gets bigger and moves down to one long nap a day, which will most likely be used for you to actually get something done around the house, it's time to establish "quiet time" for baby to give both you and baby some much-needed alone time to recharge.

My sister (who also has 4 kiddos, just a little older than mine) taught me an invaluable lesson when my first baby was tiny: You can give your baby alone time in his crib! She called it "crib time", and would put baby in his crib, along with a few favorite (safe) toys, board books, and some music playing, at some point during his awake-and-happy hours. Back in the 50's, parents used play pens for this. We lost the benefit of play pens a while back, but cribs work just as well!

Crib time offers a double benefit. In our highly-stimulated world, crib time teaches baby early on how to self-sooth and entertain himself. As my kids have gotten older, I can now tell them that I am not their on-demand party-planner. It is not my job to continuously ensure that they are occupied, engaged, and stimulated at all times (doing that would create an indulged child!). It's actually their job to *find things to do*. Remember making our own comic books back in the day? Or building a fort out of sheets, reading a book, and playing house, or cops'n'robbers, in the yard *alone*? These skills were developed in part by being allowed (or even forced) to entertain ourselves when we were little in short spurts, progressively moving on into longer independent play time.

The obvious parallel blessing in giving your Little One crib time (or independent playtime) is alone time for parent. We all have our own methods of unwinding, or "rebooting". Some need time to read, check the news, or watch a grown-up show (let's be honest, probably while folding mounds of laundry.) Some need adult stimulation, so chatting on the phone or checking in on a social media app might help you decompress and recharge. If you've got the "gift of sleep" and can snooze on-demand, take a little shut eye. You should find and do whatever appeals to you for 15 – 30 minutes (or longer if baby is happy!), enough time to regain some strength and motivation for the endless tasks of parenting ahead of you.

On a larger scale, set time aside periodically (at least once a month) to truly dis-engage from the seemingly never-ending responsibilities of the household. Date nights are essential. Time with friends (away from Little Ones) is great for re-booting, but even play-dates with another mom and her Little One will help to a.) remind you that you're not alone in this, and b.) give you some ideas and support in what you're going through (I realized early on while watching other parents that some of the "learning" I was doing was actually showing me what *not* to do. This was as valuable as learning what *to* do from other moms and dads.)

Back in the beginning (in my world, that's Genesis in the bible), our brilliant Creator initiated the Sabbath Rest for His people. He knew that after toiling for a week, His people needed some down-time to reboot and recharge. In fact, a whole day of it. I realize this may not be reasonable in our fast-paced and "busy" culture, but at least acknowledge that we were not created for constant action, tasks, and movement. Honor your body and mind's need for R&R. Protect those moments when you're recharging, and even turn off the phone and computer for a bit. Prayer and meditation, peace and silence, are highly effective de-stressors, even for just 5 minutes at a time!

Carve out the time to truly care for you. Like the airlines remind us every time we fly, put your air mask on yourself first so you'll be better equipped, energized, and oxygenated to care for those entrusted to you!

Too Good To Be True

Whatever you do with the information you've read, don't be overwhelmed and try to change or initiate everything all at once. Like I've done over the years (and continue to do!), take a nugget here, an idea there, and implement them as opportunities crop up. It may only be adding a few more reinforcers at first, and watching as your Little One responds by increasing desirable behaviors. You may try a time-out for something that in the past you let slide, but in reality you (and he) both know is not the best for anyone – like pretending to hit you or others (even pretending shows a disrespect and push at boundaries that needs correction).

I'm going to share some of the deepest core philosophies I hold with the hope that it will inspire you to evaluate what's of utmost importance to you in your parenting, and possibly help you decide which of the ideas you're sold on and plan to work toward first.

At the core of my beliefs is the conviction that there are three gifts every person is longing for and striving toward in life: ***Love, acceptance and belonging***. Unfortunately, our culture has at times taught our Little Ones that they automatically "deserve" or are "entitled" to these (just for being the most amazing child on the planet, perhaps) and they become demanding and expectant of all good things coming their way at all times. In reality, these are gifts that we *give*, and not demand be given to us.

I agree that each person is intrinsically of eternal value and worth. However, when we demand good gifts from others, by nature it's no longer a gift. Gifts are freely given and freely received. Our children, then, must be taught by our example that we are all called to *give* these good gifts – in abundance – to the world around us. In the process, we are changing our world in tiny increments, all the time. We are given the high calling of instilling in our Little Ones a desire and a roadmap to give these gifts freely back to the world.

Let me explain why I believe these 3 are the essentials.

Love is much more than a touchy, feely, sappy emotion. It's a decision to serve the needs of others, and to enrich their lives, rather than focusing on self. The greatest Teacher once said, "Greater love has no one that this: to lay down one's life for one's friends." (*New International Version,* John 15:13). He identified that love is ultimately self-sacrificing, putting the needs of another before our own. He also said, "Treat others the way you want to be treated." (paraphrased from NIV, Luke 6:31). The way you *want to be treated*, not the way you're *being* treated.

Think of Others. Get your eyes off the mirror (or the selfie-camera). Teach your Little One that he is not the center of the universe, and the goal of living just may very well be to learn how to love others selflessly, not receiving anything in return. Now I know this may seem in opposition to some of what we've laid out in this little book, as we can (and should) exemplify sacrificial love with and toward our children, but love also means *wanting the best for another.* If I want the very best for my child, I want to leave him better than I got him.

This means instilling in him the very values that are paramount to me, oftentimes helping him to re-direct his course when he's strayed from the path of virtue.

Acceptance means, "you're OK just being who you are." That doesn't mean we ignore or overlook hurtful or abusive behavior in others. It simply means that the personality, intrinsic traits, and idiosyncrasies of others are accepted. We all long to know we're "good enough". We all long to know that *even when we screw up*, we're loved. It also means overlooking the small stuff and knowing which battles to choose. Choose wisely and we have a more effective voice.

Belonging means, "you're part of this clan, and always will be." Belonging gives us a point of reference in this big, sometimes unfriendly world, where everyone longs to know who "my people" are. Why do kids come home at Christmas, even to a dysfunctional family? Because even when it's a little on the crazy side, family is still the place where we know we belong (or at least it should be!).

When we know we belong somewhere, we are given the freedom to step out into the world with confidence, knowing there's a safety-net built in when the going gets tough (and it almost always does at some point, right?). Where we belong is where we feel safe to be our truest selves, knowing that we're loved and accepted there. See how the 3 gifts are intertwined?

I have fallen short *daily* on achieving the ideals I've set forth in this little book. Ask any member of my family and they will tell you (with an ironic chuckle) that I've far too often failed to follow my own advice. And our family suffers the consequences for it (like when I challenge my husband's parenting choices in front of the kids. It doesn't go well for anyone, I can assure you).

But just because we make mistakes, even a lot of them, doesn't mean we give up trying! We press on toward the goal, knowing the prize may very well be children who are respectful, engaged, intelligent, resourceful, responsible, friendly, and kind. Not all the time, of course – we're all human and fallible! But the happiest, most functional people are those who continuously pick themselves up when mistakes are made, brush themselves off, forgive themselves and others when needed, and press on toward doing better next time.

The hope is that we, as parents, recognize that we truly do have a High Calling in that we are influencing and even building the future. One child, well-raised and given the tools to be "good" at life, can change the world. We all know it's true. Think back to that one teacher in school who made you want to be a better student, a better person. Remember that child who was always kind to the "weird" kid, and how he inspired you to take notice of the unseen and awkward others in this world.

Think of Jesus, Abraham Lincoln, Ghandi, Mother Teresa, Martin Luther King Junior. I can imagine they had some amazing examples early on in life. And each of them, though only one person, changed history.

We are truly powerful beyond imagine. We are all world-changers. Our Little Ones will be world-changers too. They are the next generation that will take care of the elderly (us, in just a few decades!), the earth, and each other. Imagine if each of us raised up just one child who infected his block or neighborhood with love, acceptance and belonging. Imagine if our Little One created the "ripple effect" in his little world that brought a bit more joy, goodness, and love, that in turn brought much-needed transformation to his neighborhood.

I'll leave you with a little story that's been inspirational to me and countless others for many generations. It's the story of the Starfish:

Once upon a time, there was an old man who used to go to the ocean to do his writing. He had a habit of walking on the beach every morning before he began his work. Early one morning, he was walking along the shore after a big storm had passed and found the vast beach littered with starfish as far as the eye could see, stretching in both directions.

Off in the distance, the old man noticed a small boy approaching. As the boy walked, he paused every so often and as he grew closer, the man could see that he was occasionally bending down to pick up an object and throw it into the sea. The boy came closer still and the man called out, "Good morning! May I ask what it is that you are doing?"

The young boy paused, looked up, and replied "Throwing starfish into the ocean. The tide has washed them up onto the beach and they can't return to the sea by themselves," the youth replied. "When the sun gets high, they will die, unless I throw them back into the water."

The old man replied, "But there must be tens of thousands of starfish on this beach. I'm afraid you won't really be able to make much of a difference."

The boy bent down, picked up yet another starfish and threw it as far as he could into the ocean. Then he turned, smiled and said, "It made a difference to that one!"

Adapted by Peter Straube (2011) from *The Starfish Thrower* by Loren Eiseley (1907 – 1977).

NOTES

Chapter 1

Dunstan, Priscilla. Calm the Crying. London: The Penguin Group, 2012. Print.

Weissbluth, Marc, M.D. *Healthy Sleep Habits, Happy Child.* New York: Random House Inc, 2015. Print.

Hogg, Tracy. *Secrets of the Baby Whisperer.* New York: Ballantine Books, 2005. Print.

Dobson, James. *The New Dare to Discipline.* Carol Stream: Tyndale Publishing, 2012. Print.

Chapter 3

Belic, Roko. (2011). *Happy,* documentary movie. United States: Roko Belic.

Chapter 4

Mc Leod, Saul. (2007). Pavlov's Dogs; Skinner – Operant Conditioning. Retrieved from https://www. simplypsychology.org.

Conclusion

New International Version Bible. Grand Rapids: Zondervan, 2002. Print.

Straube, Peter. (2011). *The Starfish Story: One step toward changing the world.* Retrieved from https:// eventsforchange.wordpress.com.

YOUR NOTES

AKNOWLEDGEMENTS

(i.e. Gushing Gratitude)

I cannot begin to thank all those who supported, encouraged, read, edited, and helped revise my words into the book you now hold.

Helen, I am forever in your debt for taking the time, in the midst of teaching a class full of antsy 3rd graders, to edit (line-by-line!) and review my book. I already deeply admired you for your love and dedication to every child you teach (including 3 of my own!), now you have taken my admiration to a whole new level.

Kristine, for being willing to read my thoughts, and offer your encouragement (and even excitement!) over the message. Your support helped me to move forward and believe that I (like you!) can offer some guidance to parents as they train up their broods.

Melinda, for offering me your time and red-pen comments so freely and honestly. You helped me to clearly define myself and my beliefs, and I know my readers will thank you for that!

Juanita, my spiritual director, my advocate, my guide. You helped me believe I have something to offer the world. I am forever grateful for your supportive, loving honesty and guidance.

Lindy, even with 2 teenagers and a tiny one toddling beside you, you lovingly scoured every word and sentence to optimize my message. Not only do you exemplify "good" parenting (amazing, in fact!), you shower the world with your boundless love.

Kate, I might tend to think you're biased because of our 41 year friendship, but in case it's NOT bias and you really ARE my biggest fan, I thank you for every word of encouragement and loving support. You pushed me forward when I wanted to stick this book (then a word doc) in a file and leave it there for my kids to find when I was long gone.

Mom and dad, how can I thank the people who raised me to be who I am today? You taught me how to love others, to respect authority, and to see the Higher Purpose in this life. Thank you for teaching me to fall madly in love with the One who created it all. You guys did good.

And to my husband Bryan, who not only encouraged (even convinced, at times!) me to stay home to raise our babies some 16 years, but continues to give me the freedom and courage to pursue my dreams. I got a good man.

And of course, to my amazing kids: Caden, Brady, Nathan and Ellie. My personal Training Grounds who get to experience first-hand every mistake, every failing, every mis-step, and every so often, those successes that have helped mold you into pretty terrific young people. I can't WAIT to see what God's got in store for you – I know it's gonna be good, my little pebble-tossing ripple-makers! I love you beyond imagine.

Printed in the United States
By Bookmasters